The Summer of '67

Jeffery Grayer

LAST DAYS OF STEAM ON THE SOUTHERN

KINGFISHER PRODUCTIONS
WATERSHED MILL, SETTLE, NORTH YORKSHIRE BD24 9LR
WWW.RAILWAYVIDEO.COM

CONTENTS PAGE

In memory of my Uncle who introduced me to steam.

ISBN 978-0-946184-69-9

All pictures by the author unless otherwise stated
© Jeffery Grayer and Kingfisher Productions 2007

Printed by The Amadeus Press, Cleckheaton

Above: Nameplate from West Country Class No. 34004 *Yeovil*

Left: Standing in the down bay platform at Southampton Cen
No. 34095 *Brentor* awaits departure with a parcels service
Weymouth.

Front Cover : A particularly impressive No. 34004 *Yeovil* spor
nameplate and crest, which was becoming an increasingly
sight by this time, leaves Southampton with a London bo
express

Rear cover: The last steam timetable for BR Southern Reg
Although the expiry date was published as 11th June 1967, it w
however, extended to 9th July owing to delays in the deliver
electric stock which gave steam a further month of life.

Introduction page: Taken from the playing fields of an adja
school, two locomotives with guards van await transportatio
South Wales lodged temporarily in a siding near Warblin
Halt to the east of Havant.

Frontipiece: Although in reasonable external condition, the r
rims of the wheels of No. 73016 seen here at Weymouth testif
the fact that this locomotive has not moved for some time. In
it was withdrawn in December 1966.

INTRODUCTION

The Summer of 1967 was know as the Summer of Love. It was a time of gatherings, happenings and love-ins. There were open air concerts at Hyde Park. One of the biggest events of the Summer was the 'Festival of Flower Children', ironically enough in the grounds of the stately home of the Duchess of Bedford, Woburn Abbey. According to the Sunday Times, it attracted over 0 hippies from all over Europe. On the other side of the Atlantic, beautiful people converged on the California coastal town of erey. The flower became the symbol of the younger generation's rebellion against their parents' values. It was everywhere; g men, as well as women, wearing flowers in their hair. It also saw the release of The Beatles' seminal album 'Sergeant Pepper's ly Hearts Club Band'. Be that as it may, of much more import to the railway enthusiast of the time was the impending demise am on the Southern Region of British Rail scheduled for 9th July.

iving in Chichester, the county town of West Sussex, during the mid 1960s, I was within easy reach of the Southern Region's from Waterloo to Southampton, Bournemouth and Weymouth and was able to capture on film the final months of operations e last steam worked mainline on the BR network. During the last twelve months of steam services I, along with hundreds of enthusiasts, visited the remaining handful of steam depots, photographed the locomotives and whenever possible travelled on n hauled trains both express and local. Looking back on my photographic collection now it is easy to wish that I had taken many shots but hindsight is a wonderful thing and one must always bear in mind that the funds of a schoolboy in the 1960s available urchasing film and travelling around the rail system were severely limited.

y the beginning of the last year of steam, July 1966, there remained just 184 survivors from a steam fleet that had numbered ust seven years before By that fateful last day, 9th July 1967, capital stock was down to just 72, so it is not surprising that many of film must have been exposed on the same dwindling band of locomotives during the final months. Pre-nationalisation es surviving on the SR at the end were limited to a few USA tanks and Bulleid Pacifics, the remainder of the fleet being made Standard types and Ivatt tanks.

couple of highlights stand out for me during this period. One was a visit to the Isle of Wight in November 1966 a few weeks e the end of steam here on 31st December, and the other was a trip on what was then billed as 'BR's Last Steam Branch', the rom Brockenhurst to Lymington made in March 1967. I along with countless others managed to tour the sheds at Weymouth, emouth, Ryde, Eastleigh, and Nine Elms although those at Guildford and Salisbury always proved that much more difficult nk'.

en when July 1967 had come and gone I was able to continue my acquaintance with SR steam for, moving to Bristol to begin a rsity course in October 1967, I was able to attend the annual Bath Road Shed Open Days in Bristol where on my first visit a le of Bulleids en route to South Wales for scrapping were exhibited. I also made visits to Weymouth and Salisbury dumping nds where the redundant steam fleet was temporarily housed until the spring of 1968 awaiting transhipment to the scrapyards. eniently it was but a relatively short hop from Bristol to the graveyard of steam at Barry and during several visits here over the ew years I was able to see again not just those types that had been active during the last year of steam operation but some that leparted this life prior to 1966 in the shape of a solitary Q type plus a variety of S15s and Maunsell moguls.

ncredibly it is now 40 years since No. 35030 *Elder Dempster Lines* entered Waterloo with the last steam hauled service, the 1407 Weymouth on 9th July 1967. Even more incredible have been the achievements of the preservation movement which has seen ss than 80 former SR steam locomotives representing 25 different classes rescued from oblivion. From that unique group that ervice during those unforgettable twelve months of the SR's Steam Swansong there remain however just nine SR and six lard and Ivatt types.

My thanks to Barry J. Eagles for providing shots of the activity during those last few hectic days of the steam service, pictures countably missing from my own collection.

y Grayer

rset
2007

USA TANKS

Above: A brace of USA tanks seen at the rear of Eastleigh in the shape of No. 30067 and Departmental Locomotive DS233, form No. 30061. No. 30067 soldiered on until the end in July 1967 but DS233, which had latterly worked at Redbridge Sleeper Depot, displaced from there by a Drewry diesel shunter in March 1967.

Below: No. 30072 at Salisbury Dump next to Standard tank No. 82029. Along with sister No. 30064, 30072 was rescued preservation and is currently based on the Keighley & Worth valley line.

e: Salisbury dump seen here in August 1967 continued to hold stock destined for the South Wales scrapyards until the final
*...*rture in March 1968. USA tanks Nos. 30064 and 30072 on the scrapline at Salisbury. No. 30064 had made its final journey in
*...*n from Eastleigh shed on Saturday 8th July 1967 coming up in tandem with No. 30071, whilst No. 30072, the last occupant of
... had made the trek across from Guildford shed.

v: 70H Ryde shed plays host to Hunslet diesel D2254, which had arrived on the island in September in connection with the
*...*coming electrification works, and O2 tank No. W22 *Brading* in this view taken in November 1966.

ISLE OF WIGHT 02s

Above: Already out of service by November 1966 and parked at the side of Ryde MPD is No. W35 with even its replacement nameplates removed. Along with Nos. W21/26/29 *Freshwater* was one of the quartet of O2s withdrawn during 1966. Whilst the other three were scrapped at Ryde Works W35 was retained for spares to keep the remaining veterans running.

Below: No. W22 *Brading* comes storming out of Ryde heading towards Smallbrook no longer a junction since the closure of the Cowes line in February 1966. The Junction signalbox closed at the end of the summer season, 17th September, as usual but this time it to be for good. Note the insulators and conductor rails already in place on this section which although having the appearance double track was in fact two single lines.

ve: No. W28 *Ashey* takes water at Ryde shed towards the end of its days. Along with 8 other surviving tanks, No. W28 was moved [N]ewport where Joliffe's scrap metal merchants did their worst in the spring of 1967. No. W31 was scrapped at Ryde Works in [Sep]tember 1967 and the sole survivor W24 *Calbourne* continues to this day on the preserved IOW Steam Railway.

w: No. W27 *Merstone* gets away from Bembridge with a Ryde train. The former Bembridge branch bay is visible on the right [a]nd the station nameboard. Note the collection of fire irons resting on the locomotive's tank top. Latterly there were just 10 O2s [rem]aining in service by the end of steam on 31st December 1966.

THE LYMINGTON BRANCH

Above: Billed as BR's "Last Steam Branch", the Brockenhurst-Lymington line of the SR succumbed to diesel traction in April 19 visited the branch on the penultimate steam weekend arriving on rebuilt WC Pacific No. 34024 *Tamar Valley.* Note the branch t waiting in the bay platform.

Below: The somewhat precarious run round loop at Lymington Pier has little apart from a flimsy buffer stop to prevent the unw driver from ending up in the drink. Standard and Ivatt tanks shared duties latterly on this branch having taken over from the serving M7s in 1964. Withdrawal of the Drummonds required the practice of running round at the end of each trip to be reinsta the more modern traction not being push-pull fitted

e: Having run round its train, No. 80152 waits to return to the junction. April 2nd 1967 saw the final steam workings with Ivatt No. 41320 in charge. A 3 car Hampshire DMU took over services the following day in the interim until electrification was pleted the following month. The electric service still operates today with "Heritage" slam door stock.

v: Between trips, the rostered locomotive of the day, a very presentable Standard Tank No. 80152, takes water at a column on the er Ringwood branch bay at Brockenhurst.

Aove: Although signalled away, a member of the footplate crew is talking on the 'phone to Southampton Box as No. 34023 *Black[more] Vale* waits at Central station to take over the next leg of a special train run on 3rd June 1967 utilising preserved A4 Pacific 449[8] *Nigel Gresley*. The Bulleid ran from Southampton to Salisbury via Eastleigh whence No. 4498 took over again for the run bac[k to] Waterloo.

Below: Outflanked by replacement motive power in the shape of a green liveried Hampshire demu and the new all-blue electric s[tock,] No. 34023 *Blackmore Vale* gets away from Southampton with a Bournemouth train.

ve: The white painted smokebox hinges and lamp brackets cannot disguise the very grimy condition of *Blackmore Vale* as its
...ds outside Eastleigh shed minus tender. No. 34023 was one of the final pair of unmodified Bulleids, with No. 34102, to see out
...m on the SR subsequently being purchased for preservation for the sum of £1,900 in 1967.

...w: A visitor from 70A, No. 34002 *Salisbury* has managed to retain its nameplate under all that grime as it rests outside Eastleigh
...ot in early 1967. It was withdrawn in April and after periods of storage at Nine Elms and Salisbury was scrapped at Cashmores
...d in Newport in October of that year.

Above: Eastleigh based No. 34102 *Lapford* in very presentable condition brings an engineer's train past Southampton Central Many a former express engine was used on relatively lowly engineering and goods trains latterly, many of the former ru connection with the forthcoming electrification of the Bournemouth line.

Below: Eastleigh shed plays host to No. 34102 *Lapford* still sporting its embellishments of whitened buffers, brake hoses, lamp brac and smokebox hinges with which many a locomotive was adorned when hauling enthusiasts' specials.

e: Under the impressive signal gantry at the west end of Southampton Central station No. 34001 *Exeter* leaves with a Weymouth whilst No. 34036 *Westward Ho* waits time in the bay platform with a Bournemouth stopper.

w: With nameplate and crest, although in an altogether grubby state, is *Okehampton* at the London end of Southampton Central. 34013 was one of the band of 17 rebuilt Bulleid light pacifics that lasted in service until 9th July 1967.

Above: Hauling the returning leg of the LCGB "Vectis Farewell" special of 31st December 1966, No. 34013 *Okehampton* is held signals in the fading winter light outside Chichester station. Tour participants had started the day behind No. 73065 double hea with 73043 from Waterloo, had sampled Isle of Wight steam behind Nos. W17/22/24/31, and were finishing the day in fine s with a run from Portsmouth Harbour to Waterloo via the Mid Sussex line.

Above: Departing Woking past the rather ornate shop frontages to the right No. 34021 *Dartmoor* makes for the capital with a s semi-fast service. Like so many of its classmates, No. 34021 ended its days at Cashmores scrapyard in Newport which wa despatch no fewer than 38 of Bulleid's light pacifics and five of the Merchant Navy class.

e: No. 34021 awaits attention alongside a increasingly decrepit Nine Elms shed.

e: A steam shrouded *Tamar Valley* starts away from the Winchester stop with a London train. No. 34024 which had the honour rking the last down steam hauled 'Bournemouth Belle' on July 5th, ran only 150,000 miles, the lowest achieved by any rebuild, e six years five months between modification in February 1961 and withdrawal in July 1967.

Above: No. 34024 *Tamar Valley* has the road prior to its departure for London, a journey which, with delays caused by electrific
engineering works, was often protracted to 100 minutes or more from Southampton, the best time of 93 minutes being allowe
the 1030 down and the Bournemouth Belle . Notwithstanding this, some very fast times were recorded during the last twelve m
of steam running by drivers willing to "have a go".

Below: Nos. 34037 *Clovelly* and 34040 *Crewkerne* pose outside Eastleigh shed. The former retains its nameplate backing plate b
became increasingly the case with the end of steam approaching, its nameplate had been removed for safe keeping and subse
sale.

e: The NE coach behind No. 34040 *Crewkerne* confirms the fact that this was an inter-regional service from Poole – York. The
an has "the bag in" and will no doubt wish to ensure a tender full of water is obtained to see the pacific through to its next
duled water stop.

e: The traditional knotted handkerchief garb of many footplate crew is seen as No. 34044 *Woolacombe*, with safety valves lifting,
es Southampton Central. After less than 21 years' service this locomotive was withdrawn in May 1967.

Above: An open firebox door reveals the blaze at the heart of No. 34047 *Callington* resting on Eastleigh shed. This locomotive withdrawn just before the end of steam working in June.

Below: In this view taken at Eastleigh shed amid the piles of ash and debris, a trio of light pacifics comprising Nos. 34060 *25 Squa* 34037 *Clovelly* and 34040 *Crewkerne* is on display. Once again only the backing plate on No. 34060 is apparent, the nameplate squadron crest having already been removed.

e: Apparently still good for many more years but the disconnected motion says it all. No. 34071 *601 Squadron* is being prepared ...stleigh for towing to Cashmores scrapyard at Newport where it was promptly cut up in September 1967.

v: A Salisbury resident since September 1963, 34089 *602 Squadron* on its home shed still sports traces of the high standard of ...motive turnout that characterised Salisbury shed. On the right are several trucks on the ramp that fed the coal shute.

Above: The light pacific which formerly carried the longest nameplate, *Sir Eustace Missenden – Southern Railway* is turned on Bournemouth turntable. No. 34090, never one of the more popular steeds with footplate crews, was dumped at Salisbury February 1968 whence it departed for Cashmores at Newport.

Above: No. 34095 *Brentor* negotiates the yard at the rear of Eastleigh shed passing Standard Class 5 No. 73117 formerly named *V* No. 34095 was stored at Weymouth after withdrawal until forming part of the final convoy of locomotives to be towed from 70 January 1968 to South Wales for scrapping.

ve: A particularly dirty specimen in the form of 34104 *Bere Alston* brakes sharply past Southampton Central box before coming
halt in the up main platform with a Waterloo train.

w: No. 34108 *Wincanton* enters Southampton Central passing the former power station, the lowering sun highlighting the white
ted smokebox door hinges. The old power station dominates the right-hand side of the picture.

Above: One of the seven Merchant Navy Class which lasted until July 1967, *Royal Mail* is seen in the yard at Weymouth. At the of 1967 Weymouth had 10 of these machines on its strength but all, including No. 35003, were transferred to Nine Elms in Febr to see out their remaining months. A corner of the turntable pit can just be seen in this view.

Below: Reduced to semi-fast working, No. 35007 *Aberdeen Commonwealth* shuffles away leaking steam from Branksome w Weymouth service in a pale reflection of former top link workings.

ve: 35008 *Orient Line* draws up at Southampton Central, then in the throes of rebuilding, with a London train. No. 35008 was in
ration right up to the last week of steam being noted on the 12:34 Bournemouth – Waterloo service on July 7th.

w: 35012 *United States Line* stands amid the debris in the roofless area known as the "Old Shed" next to the "New Shed" at Nine
s in an area to be made famous in David Shepherd's painting "Nine Elms – The Last Hours".

Above: 35013 *Blue Funnel* negotiates the tricky ascent from the coal shute road at Nine Elms shed prior to backing down to Wate
to work a Bournemouth train.

Below: The water crane chain hanging over the tender side indicates that the opportunity is being taken to refill the tender of
35013 *Blue Funnel* during a stop at Southampton Central. The magnificent signal gantry outlasted steam only to be demolished s
years later as part of the Southampton Area resignalling scheme.

ve: A red 'Not to be Moved' board is attached to the tender of one of a trio of locomotives seen at Weymouth shed, then coded
No. 35014 *Nederland Line* is prominent in this view and was withdrawn in March 1967 before being stored for a few months at
mouth prior to despatch to South Wales for scrapping.

v: Bournemouth shed yard sees No. 35028 *Clan Line* with steam to spare and nameplates still in place. This was the only
chant Navy to be preserved straight from BR service which, in company with No. 34023 *Blackmore Vale,* was stored temporarily
ine Elms after steam traction finished.

Above: Fittingly the final Merchant Navy in numerical sequence, No. 35030 *Elder Demps Lines* seen here at the head of a London service Southampton, was to bring the final steam haul arrival into Waterloo, the 1407 from Weymou on July 9th.

IVATT TANKS

Left: No. 41224 is seen in Bournemouth shed ya Latterly used on the Lymington branchline, the tanks performed a variety of shunting, ecs a goods duties until the end of steam.

ve: No. 41224 is one of the pair of Ivatts, the other being No. 41320, which lasted in service at Bournemouth shed until July 1967.

w: The driver removes the lamps from the coaching set which is in the charge of No. 41224 at Swanage shortly before the demu over of September 1966.

Above: No. 41301 parked at the side of Weymouth shed was withdrawn in September 1966 and is seen with a goods wagon dedic
to "Weymouth MPD" use.

Below: No. 41298 has just come off the turntable seen in the background at Nine Elms shed whilst Standard tank No. 820
following suit.

STANDARD CLASSES

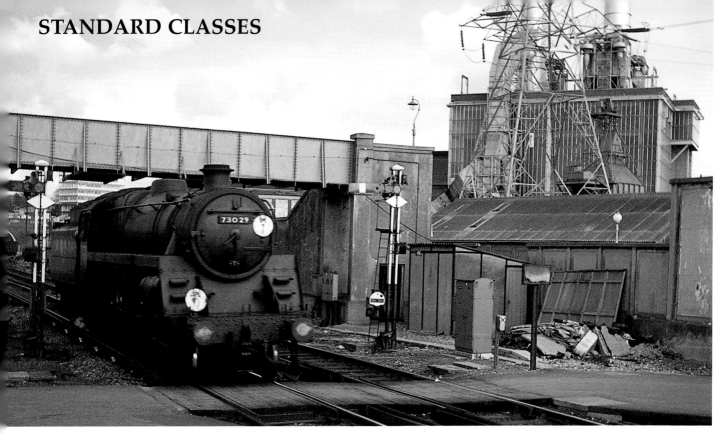

ove: No. 73029 runs light engine through Southampton Central. This locomotive was one of ten Standard Class 5s which saw out ·am on the Southern Region.

low: Prior to getting away from the down bay at Southampton Central, a member of the footplate crew leans out of the cab window ·filthy Standard Class 5 No. 73018 to check the signal aspect.

Above: The tender of No. 73020 is filled during the station stop at Southampton whilst the sun shines onto the faded moqu[ette] upholstery of the first compartment of a green Bulleid coach at the head of the train.

Below: The barest minimum of cleaning, just enough to reveal the running number, has been done on No. 73037 seen simme[ring] quietly in front of Eastleigh shed.

e: No. 73037 waits for clearance at the east end of Southampton Central en route to Eastleigh for servicing. Great change is taking
. to the buildings on Platform 1 with the old station buildings demolished, the site awaits the erection of the new structure, now
vn as Overline House.

y: With Radipole Lake in the background an unidentified Standard Class 5 drops down into Weymouth with a local working
. Bournemouth.

Above: The sun glints off the rods of an unidentified Standard Class 5 as it rounds the curve into Southampton Central with an u[...] passing a stationary Hampshire dmu.

Below: The sunlight catches the side of a very unkempt No. 73117 *Vivien* at Eastleigh shed. No. 73117 lasted in service until Marc[...]

e: The coaling stage is the setting for No. 73117 *Vivien* as it is refuelled during servicing at Weymouth depot.

v: A quartet of condemned Standards, including No. 73171, with rods removed and motion tied up ready for towing, await the call at Eastleigh depot.

Above: The Eastleigh water tower and coaling stage are seen in this view of No. 75075 being serviced between turns. 75075 was of four of this class of Standard 4 4-6-0 that lasted in service until July 1967.

Below: Scuttling through Southampton Central light engine is Standard Class 4 No. 76011. The skyline is dominated by the v tank, Civic Centre clock tower and the Gaumont Theatre.

e: Eastleigh based No. 76066 gets away from Southampton with a down stopping train for Bournemouth. This was one of 10 dard 4 2-6-0s which remained in service until July.

v: With rusting boiler cladding No. 76033 stands out of steam at the rear of Eastleigh shed. It was withdrawn in February 1967.

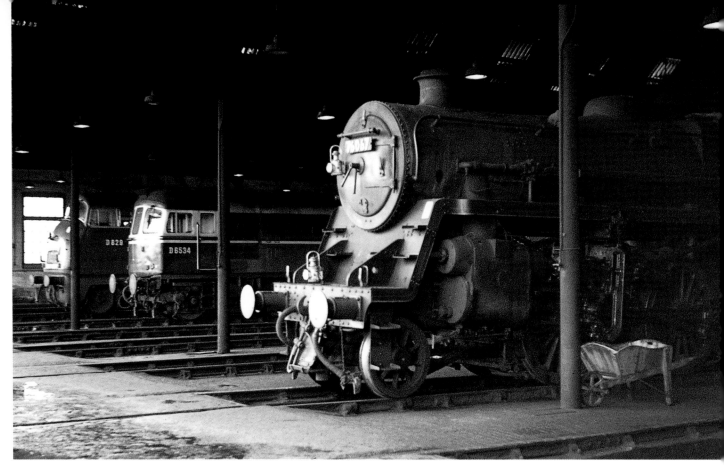

Above: One of the few occasions when I managed to get round Salisbury shed undetected, Standard Class 4 No. 76067 rests along
Crompton D6534 and maroon liveried Warship diesel D829 *Magpie*. The wheelbarrow is typical of the "shed furniture" of the pe

Below: An unidentified Standard Class 4 2-6-0 gets away from Southampton Central with a stopping service to Bournemouth.

e: The unique No. 77014, the only Standard Class 3 4-6-0 to be based on the Southern Region, is seen at its home shed of dford. This locomotive does have a claim to be the last steam locomotive to undertake revenue earning duty on the SR when it ered a van train from Bournemouth into Weymouth on the evening of 9th July.

v: Unceremoniously dumped at Weymouth with rods removed, No. 77014 awaits the inevitable in company with other ndant motive power.

Above: One of Bournemouth's trio of Standard tanks which lasted until July, No. 80011, is at rest in the shed yard.

Below: No. 80133 calls at Southampton Central with a stopper to Eastleigh. The new buildings on Platform 1 are progressing.

e: An unidentified Standard tank departs Southampton with a Bournemouth stopping service.

v: Standard Class 3MT No. 82029 at Nine Elms shed was used primarily for ecs duties at Waterloo. Along with No. 82019 this continued in service here until July 1967 finding its way to Salisbury dump for storage prior to disposal for scrapping.

FINALE

Above: On the 18th June 1967 Wareham plays host to Nos. 34108 *Wincanton* and 34089 *602 Squadron* double heading an RCTS sp
which saw six different locomotives hauling the train during the day. No. 80146 replaced 34108 at Wareham for a run over
Swanage branch
Below: No. 34089 *602 Squadron* waits at Fareham to take over the Southampton leg of the RCTS special of 18th June 1967 from
34023 *Blackmore Vale* and No. 73029 which had brought it from Waterloo.   *Both, Barry J. Eagles*

e: It is 30th June 1967
No. 35003 *Royal Mail*
into its stride passing
on on the outskirts of
hampton.

t: On 21st June 1967
73037 hurries a train
gh the New Forest
Ashurst. On the right
e track can be seen one
e famous 'You're in the
g Country'
ertisement hoardings of
g's brewery of Romsey.
Barry J. Eagles

Above: No. 34052 *Lord Dowding* at Redbridge on 3rd July 1967 has charge of a freight service consisting of banana vans. It was to appear on one of the last steam hauled freights, the 1420 Weymouth – Westbury tomatoes, on the 9th July.

Below: On 3rd July 1967 No. 34025 *Whimple* crosses the River Test west of Southampton with the up Bournemouth Belle. On this No. 34025 hauled both down and up Belles, the last steam operated Belles running just two days later with Nos. 34024 and 3 respectively.   *Both, Barry J. Eagles*

e: Sporting reinstated nameplates, a specially cleaned No. 35008 *Orient Line* coasts into Southampton Central with the down BR well to Southern Steam Special No. 1 of 2nd July 1967. Originally it had been planned to run five such specials but in the event two were operated.

v: One week before the end of steam Southampton's crowded platforms say it all as No. 35028 *Clan Line* comes to a halt with the R Farewell Special No. 2 on 2nd July priced at the then outrageous fare of £4 return !   *Both, Barry J. Eagles*

AWAITING DISPOSAL

Above: A Bulleid Pacific, of which there were 8 examples stored at Weymouth in the middle of July, waits for the end between a co[uple] of BR Standards.

Below: A selection of front ends seen on the storage sidings at Weymouth depot following the end of steam working. Never hol[ding] as much as the other storage facility at Salisbury, the maximum number of locomotives taking up temporary residence here [was] approximately 25. The site was cleared of redundant stock by the end of January 1968.

e: A pair of Ivatts, Nos. 41230 and 41295, which were withdrawn in April 1967, are seen on Weymouth dump. Five of these useful
...land region imports lasted in service until the end in July with two of their number reaching preservation

v: A pair of Standard tanks, Nos. 80133 and 80152 with USA tank No. 30071 and Standard tank No. 80146 ahead of the latter,
...fit for further duty outside Salisbury shed. However, this is September 1967 and steam has already been dead for two months
...he Southern Region, only the final journey awaits these machines.

Above: No. 80016 stands amongst the rosebay willowherb at Salisbury storage sidings.

Below: Whilst a Crompton diesel busies itself with ecs movements in the background, Standard tank No. 80016 is at the buffer s on one of the redundant stock stabling sidings in front of Salisbury shed. It is flanked on the left by No. 34056 *Croydon* and USA No. 30064.

ve: No. 80151 and two further Standards lie amongst the weeds at Salisbury storage sidings. Four locomotives were to be rescued
preservation from the sidings here, two USA tanks Nos. 30064 and 30072, Ivatt tank No. 41312 and No. 80151 itself.

w: Thanks to Dai Woodham one could still enjoy the sight of SR locomotives that had been withdrawn well before the July 1967
dline. S15 No. 30499 is looking very much the worse for wear after prolonged exposure to the salt laden Barry air. Urie designed
30499 was rescued in 1983 by the Urie Locomotive Society and was moved to the Mid Hants railway.

FOR SCRAP

Above: Maunsell designed No. 30841 which was withdrawn in January 1964 spent eight years at Barry before moving in 197
Chappel & Wakes Colne initially followed by a spell at the Nene Valley. It is currently to be found on the North Yorkshire Moors
as No. 30825 reflecting its new frames provided by a sister locomotive.

Below: No. 30847 receiving attention, to prevent further corrosion, from members of the Maunsell Locomotive Society who purcha
it for £9,000 plus VAT in September 1978. It was moved to the Bluebell Railway in October of that year, being the 95th departure f
Woodham's Yard.

e: U Class mogul No. 31618 is one of 4 members of the class preserved. Withdrawn in January 1964 this was only the second motive to escape from Barry being purchased in January 1969 by the Southern Mogul Preservation Society for £2,000. After a on the KESR it was moved by road to the Bluebell Railway in 1977.

v: Minus chimney and tender U Class No. 31638 awaits rescue at Barry. The call did not come until August 1980 and it is now found on the Bluebell Railway attached to a former Schools Class tender.

Above: The sole representative of Maunsell's N Class which has been rescued, No. 31874, left Barry in March 1974 for the Mid H
Railway where it steamed for the first time in preservation in October 1976.

Below: A vivid covering of rust adorns No. 34028 *Eddystone* as it waits on the exit roads at Barry at the start of the long journe
restoration to full working order. It is currently based on the Bluebell Railway.

e: Cab to cab, 35022 *Holland America Line* and No. 34101 *Hartland* have both subsequently been saved, the former was on the *nage* line but has now been acquired by Jeremy Hosking and is based at Southall. The latter has steamed again in preservation *ne* Great Central at Loughborough but is currently based on the North York Moors line

v left: Cabside view of the remains of No. 34046 *Braunton* Thje locomotive has just been steamed once again on the West Somerset *being one of millionaire Jeremy Hosking's stable of locomotives.

v right: A raw wound on the side of No. 35018 *British India Line* reveals the remains of the boiler lagging.

Above: Hijacked en route to South Wales for scrapping, 2 rebuilt Bulleid Pacifics pose in the rain at Bath Road Open Day on October 1967. No. 34013 *Okehampton* and No. 34100 *Appledore* had both survived until the end of steam on the SR and w subsequently scrapped at Cashmores yard in Newport. *Below:* The restoration of No. 34016 *Bodmin*, seen at the rear of Alres station, in company with N Class No. 31874, undergoing initial attention. Compare this view with the one opposite!

Above: Hard to believe that the splendour which is currently the operational *Tangmere* was once in such a state. No. 34067 carries the usual daubed pleas "Please Don't Remove Parts" and "Reserved" in the often vain hope that the scavengers would leave the hulks alone. Dai Woodham estimated that hundreds of thousands of pounds worth of parts were stolen from his stock over the years and seeing the state of some of the wrecks one could well believe it !

Below: The beautifully restored West Country Class *Bodmin* which re-entered traffic in 1979, is seen hauling a train at Alresford.

SOUTHERN REGION STEAM WITHDRAWALS
JULY 1966 – JULY 1967

TOTAL CAPITAL STOCK STEAM LOCOMOTIVES   184 JULY 1966

TOTAL REMAINING AT THE END OF STEAM   72 9th JULY 1967

BOLD TYPE IN SERVICE UNTIL END OF STEAM 9 JULY 1967

		WITHDRAWN
USA TANKS		
TOTAL 6 (JULY 1966) 5 (9/7/67)		
30064*		JULY 1967
30067		JULY 1967
30069		JULY 1967
30071		JULY 1967
30072*		JULY 1967
30073		JANUARY 1967
ISLE OF WIGHT 02 TANKS		
TOTAL 11 (JULY 1966) 0 (9/7/67)		
W14	FISHBOURNE	JANUARY 1967
W16	VENTNOR	JANUARY 1967
W17	SEAVIEW	JANUARY 1967
W20	SHANKLIN	JANUARY 1967
W22	BRADING	JANUARY 1967
W24*	CALBOURNE	MARCH 1967
W27	MERSTONE	JANUARY 1967
W28	ASHEY	JANUARY 1967
W31	CHALE	MARCH 1967
W33	BEMBRIDGE	JANUARY 1967
W35	FRESHWATER	OCTOBER 1966

WEST COUNTRY/BATTLE OF BRITAIN PACIFICS
UNMODIFIED TOTAL   8 (JULY 1966) 2 (9.7.67)

34002	SALISBURY	APRIL 1967
34006	BUDE	MARCH 1967
34015	EXMOUTH	APRIL 1967
34019	BIDEFORD	MARCH 1967
34023*	BLACKMORE VALE	JULY 1967
34057	BIGGIN HILL	MAY 1967
34066	SPITFIRE	SEPTEMBER 1966
34102	LAPFORD	JULY 1967

MODIFIED TOTAL   36 (JULY 1966) 17 (9.7.67)

34001	EXETER	JULY 1967
34004	YEOVIL	JULY 1967
34005	BARNSTAPLE	OCTOBER 1966
34008	PADSTOW	JUNE 1967
34009	LYME REGIS	OCTOBER 1966
34012	LAUNCESTON	DECEMBER 1966
34013	OKEHAMPTON	JULY 1967
34017	ILFRACOMBE	OCTOBER 1966
34018	AXMINSTER	JULY 1967
34021	DARTMOOR	JULY 1967

		WITHDRAWN
34024	TAMAR VALLEY	JULY 1967
34025	WHIMPLE	JULY 1967
34026	YES TOR	SEPTEMBER 1966
34032	CAMELFORD	OCTOBER 1966
34034	HONITON	JULY 1967
34036	WESTWARD HO	JULY 1967
34037	CLOVELLY	JULY 1967
34040	CREWKERNE	JULY 1967
34044	WOOLACOMBE	MAY 1967
34047	CALLINGTON	JUNE 1967
34052	LORD DOWDING	JULY 1967
34056	CROYDON	MAY 1967
34060	25 SQUADRON	JULY 1967
34071	601 SQUADRON	APRIL 1967
34077	603 SQUADRON	MARCH 1967
34087	145 SQUADRON	JULY 1967
34088	213 SQUADRON	MARCH 1967
34089	602 SQUADRON	JULY 1967
34090	SIR EUSTANCE MISSENDEN	
	SOUTHERN RAILWAY	JULY 1967
34093	SAUNTON	JULY 1967
34095	BRENTOR	JULY 1967
34098	TEMPLECOMBE	JUNE 1967
34100	APPLEDORE	JULY 1967
34101*	HARTLAND	JULY 1966
34104	BERE ALSTON	JUNE 1967
34108	WINCANTON	JUNE 1967

MERCHANT NAVY PACIFICS   TOTAL
14 (JULY 1966)   6 (9/7/67)

35003	ROYAL MAIL	JULY 1967
35007	ABERDEEN	
	COMMONWEALTH	JULY 1967
35008	ORIENT LINE	JULY 1967
35010*	BLUE STAR	SEPTEMBER 1966
35012	UNITED STATES LINE	APRIL 1967
35013	BLUE FUNNEL	JULY 1967
35014	NEDERLAND LINE	MARCH 1967
35017	BELGIAN MARINE	JULY 1966
35023	HOLLAND-AFRIKA LINE	JULY 1967
35026	LAMPORT & HOLT LINE	MARCH 1967
35027*	PORT LINE	SEPTEMBER 1966
35028*	CLAN LINE	JULY 1967
35029*	ELLERMAN LINES	SEPTEMBER 1966
35030	ELDER DEMPSTER LINES	JULY 1967

T TANKS
AL 13 (JULY 1966)   5 (9/7/67)

4	JULY 1967
0	APRIL 1967
4	MARCH 1967
7	JULY 1966
4	SEPTEMBER 1966
5	APRIL 1967
8*	JULY 1967
9	OCTOBER 1966
1	SEPTEMBER 1966
2*	JULY 1967
6	OCTOBER 1966
9	JULY 1967
0	JULY 1967

STANDARD CLASSES   CLASS 5MT 4-6-0
AL   28 (JULY 1966)   10 (9/7/67)

2		MARCH 1967
6		DECEMBER 1966
8		JULY 1967
0		JULY 1967
2		APRIL 1967
9		JULY 1967
7		JULY 1967
3		JULY 1967
5		JULY 1967
0	MERLIN	DECEMBER 1966
1	EXCALIBUR	JULY 1966
3	PENDRAGON	SEPTEMBER 1966
5	MELISANDE	JULY 1967
6	THE GREEN KNIGHT	OCTOBER 1966
7	LINETTE	OCTOBER 1966
8	JOYOUS GARD	OCTOBER 1966
9	MAID OF ASTOLAT	SEPTEMBER 1966
2		JULY 1967
3		JULY 1967
0	THE RED KNIGHT	JANUARY 1967
3	LYONNESSE	JANUARY 1967
5	KING PELLINORE	MARCH 1967
7	VIVIEN	MARCH 1967
8	KING LEODEGRANCE	JULY 1967
9	ELAINE	MARCH 1967
5		JULY 1967
9		OCTOBER 1966
1		OCTOBER 1966

CLASS 4MT 4-6-0
TOTAL 10 (JULY 1966)   4 (9/7/67)

75065	SEPTEMBER 1966
75068	JULY 1967
75069*	SEPTEMBER 1966
75070	SEPTEMBER 1966
75074	JULY 1967
75075	JULY 1967
75076	JULY 1967
75077	JULY 1967
75078*	JULY 1966
75079*	NOVEMBER 1966

CLASS 4MT   2-6-0
TOTAL 25 (JULY 1966) 10 (9/7/67)

76005	JULY 1967
76006	JULY 1967
76007	JULY 1967
76008	MAY 1967
76009	JULY 1967
76010	SEPTEMBER 1966
76011	JULY 1967
76012	SEPTEMBER 1966
76013	SEPTEMBER 1966
76014	SEPTEMBER 1966
76016	OCTOBER 1966
76018	OCTOBER 1966
76026	JULY 1967
76031	JULY 1967
76033	FEBRUARY 1967
76053	JANUARY 1967
76057	OCTOBER 1966
76058	MARCH 1967
76059	SEPTEMBER 1966
76061	JANUARY 1967
76063	APRIL 1967
76064	JULY 1967
76066	JULY 1967
76067	JULY 1967
76069	JUNE 1967

t Country' Class No. 34102 *Lapford* prepares to rt from Southampton's Eastern Docks. *Lapford* the honour of being the very last unrebuilt ic in service on 9th July.

Barry J. Eagles

CLASS 3MT   2-6-0
TOTAL 1 (JULY 1966)   1 (9/1/67)

77014   JULY 1967

CLASS 4MT   2-6-4T
TOTAL 26 (JULY 1966)   10 (9/1/67)

80011   JULY 1967
80012   MARCH 1967
80015   JULY 1967
80016   JULY 1967
80019   MARCH 1967
80032   JANUARY 1967
80033   OCTOBER 1966
80065   SEPTEMBER 1966
80068   OCTOBER 1966
80082   SEPTEMBER 1966
80083   AUGUST 1966
80085   JUNE 1967
80089   OCTOBER 1966
80094   JULY 1966
80095   OCTOBER 1966

80133   JULY 1967
80134   JULY 1967
80138   OCTOBER 1966
80139   JULY 1967
80140   JULY 1967
80143   JULY 1967
80145   JUNE 1967
80146   JULY 1967
80151*   MAY 1967
80152   JULY 1967
80154   APRIL 1967

CLASS 3MT   2-6-2T
TOTAL 6 (JULY 1966)   2 (9/7/67)

82006   SEPTEMBER 1966
82018   JULY 1966
82019   JULY 1967
82023   OCTOBER 1966
82028   SEPTEMBER 1966
82029   JULY 1967

* TOTAL PRESERVED FROM SR FLEET OF 1966/67 =

Green liveried No. 73029 has the road from Brockenhurst with a London train.